Every Kid's Guide to
Laws that Relate to
School and Work

Written by
JOY BERRY

CHILDRENS PRESS ®
CHICAGO

About the Author and Publisher

Joy Berry's mission in life is to help families cope with everyday problems and to help children become competent, responsible, happy individuals. To achieve her goal, she has written over two hundred self-help books for children from birth through age twelve. Her work revolutionized children's publishing by providing families with practical, how-to, living skills information that was previously unavailable in children's books.

Joy gathered a dedicated team of experts, including psychologists, educators, child developmentalists, writers, editors, designers, and artists, to form her publishing company and to help produce her work.

The company, Living Skills Press, produces thoroughly researched books and audio-visual materials that successfully combine humor and education to teach subjects ranging from how to clean a bedroom to how to resolve problems and get along with other people.

Managing Editor: Ellen Klarberg
Copy Editor: Kate Dickey
Contributing Editors: Nancy Cochran, Barbara Detrich, Frank Elia,
Bob Gillen, Kathleen McBride,
Susan Motycka, Gary Passarino
Editorial Assistant: Sandy Passarino

Art Director: Laurie Westdahl
Design: Abigail Johnston, Laurie Westdahl
Production: Abigail Johnston
Illustrations designed by: Bartholomew
Inker: Berenice Happe Iriks
Colorer: Berenice Happe Iriks
Composition: Curt Chelin

There are special laws that apply to children.

In **EVERY KID'S GUIDE TO LAWS THAT RELATE TO SCHOOL AND WORK**, you will learn the following:
- some laws are specifically for children,
- some school laws protect and help children,
- some school laws protect and help principals and teachers, and
- children's labor laws protect and help children.

Because you are a child, you are a *minor.* A minor is a person below a certain age who is under the guidance of his or her parents or guardians.

The *age of majority* (the age at which you stop being a minor) varies from state to state. In some states you are a minor until you become 18. In other states you are a minor until you become 21.

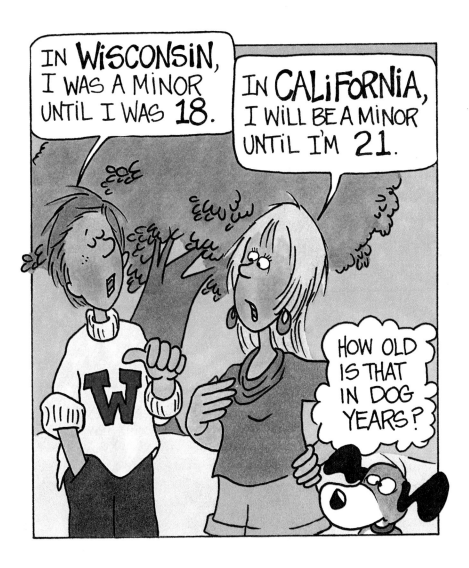

Often children think that because they are minors, they are not responsible for following the law. This is not true.

Children under six years of age are not considered intelligent enough to be responsible for the law, but this is not true of children seven years of age and older. Minors over seven years of age are expected to obey the law.

If you are like most children, you do not know about the laws you are supposed to obey. This is because very little has been written for children about the laws that relate to them. There is a lot of information about laws for teenagers and young adults, but not much has been written for children.

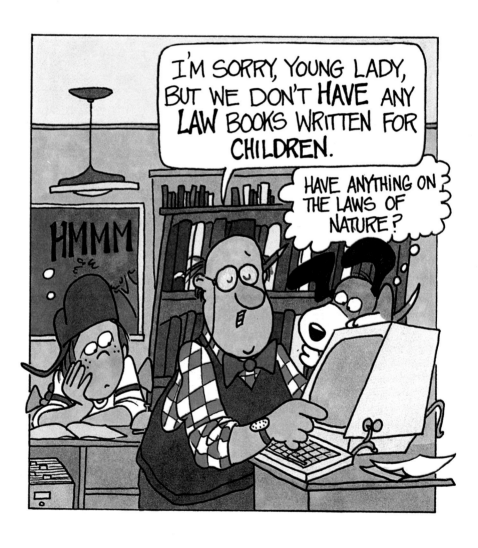

This book is for children. It doesn't deal with *all* of the laws that apply to minors. Instead, it deals with the school and labor laws that apply to minors between the ages of seven and thirteen.

In regard to the laws that relate to you at school, each state decides

- what age a child must be to begin school,
- what age he or she must be to quit school, and
- what students will study at school.

States also decide what a person must do in order to become a principal or a teacher.

Each district has a **_Board of Education_** (a group of people who is in charge of overseeing the schools in its district).

The Board of Education
- **_provides the curriculum_** (what the students are taught) for each school,
- **_establishes the rules_** for each school, and
- **_hires principals and teachers_** to enforce the rules.

Some of the laws that relate to you at school have been established to protect you. According to the law, *every* child between six or seven and sixteen years of age is entitled to a free education.

Therefore, you must attend a public school full time from the time you are six or seven until you graduate from high school, unless

- a mental or physical problem makes it impossible for you to attend school,
- you attend a private school,
- you receive private instruction from a credentialed instructor,
- your parents or guardians conduct school for you at home,
- you receive vocational training at a place of employment and attend continuation classes several hours a week, or
- you live far away from the school and have no transportation to and from school.

It would be difficult, if not impossible, for your principal and teachers to educate you if you did not go to school. Therefore, it is against the law for you to be absent from school without a valid (real) excuse.

You are *truant* when you have several unexcused absences. You are considered a *habitual truant* when you continue to miss school without valid reasons. According to the law, habitual truants can be arrested.

According to the law, your principal and teachers are "in loco parentis." This means that they are like your parents or guardians when you are in school. As "in loco parentis", your principal and teachers must do everything they can to see that you are kept healthy and safe during the hours you are in school.

As "in loco parentis", your principal and teachers must *control* you. They must do everything they can to see that you do not harm yourself or other people and their property while you are in school.

It is against the law for your principal and teachers to *neglect* you. If your principal and teachers fail to protect and control you, they are neglecting you and therefore disobeying the law.

It is against the law for your principal and teachers to abuse you. They cannot do *anything* that will injure you. This includes mental, physical, and sexual abuse.

Sometimes it is hard to know whether or not a principal or teacher has neglected or abused a child. It is especially hard for children to determine this by themselves. Parents or guardians can help children decide whether a principal or teacher has neglected or abused them.

If you feel that you are being neglected or abused, talk to your parents or guardians about it. Do not lie or exaggerate. It will be extremely difficult for your parents or guardians to help you if you do not tell the truth.

If your principal or teacher has not neglected or abused you, your parents or guardians can assure you of that fact and help you understand why your principal or teacher did what he or she did. If your principal or teacher has neglected or abused you, your parents or guardians might be able to do something to make sure it never happens again.

You, like all other citizens of the United States, are entitled to the protection and basic freedoms contained in the Constitution of the United States.

Because of your constitutional rights, you are entitled to *due process of the law.* This means that you can do whatever the law allows to make sure that your constitutional rights to *life, liberty, and the pursuit of happiness* are not being abused or taken away.

One very important freedom provided by the
Constitution is *freedom of expression.* Schools must
respect this freedom by allowing you to "express
yourself" (share your views, beliefs, and concerns) as
long as the way you express yourself does not
interfere with the work and discipline of the school.

In regard to your *personal appearance,* according to the law, you may dress and wear your hair as you and your parents or guardians see fit as long as your clothes and hairstyle do not interfere with the work and discipline of the school.

In regard to **student records** (files containing student grades, test scores, and written comments by school personnel), the law states that

- up until you are 18, your parents or guardians can see any of your records. No one else (except school authorities and police officials) can see your records unless they are given written permission to do so by your parents or guardians; and

- after you are 18, only *you* (along with school authorities and police officials) can see your records. Others can see your records only if *you* give them written permission to do so.

You and your parents or guardians can petition (request) to have any material removed from your record that is damaging or not proved. The school might or might not do as you request. If the school refuses your request, they must put a statement in your file explaining that you disagreed with the record and requested that it be changed.

Some of the laws that relate to you at school have been established to help your principal and teacher do their jobs.

According to the law, your principal and teacher can do whatever is necessary to provide a free and adequate education for their students.

Therefore, principals and teachers have a right to establish school and classroom rules in addition to the ones established by the Board of Education.

Although the law does not give children the right to make school and classroom rules, most principals and teachers would agree that students are more committed to obeying the rules if they have taken part in making them.

If the children in your school do not have any part in making the rules, talk to your principal and teacher about it. Talking to them might lead to more student involvement in making the school rules.

According to the law, principals and teachers are responsible for enforcing school and classroom rules. To help them enforce the rules, the law gives your principal and teacher the right to **discipline** you. Principals and teachers must have a **good cause** for disciplining their students, and the discipline must be **reasonable.**

Your principal and teacher, whenever necessary, can *punish* you. In some states this includes physical punishment. In other states physical punishment is forbidden.

Whenever necessary, your principal or teacher can *suspend* you from the classroom or the school. This means that you stay out of your classroom for several days.

Your principal and teacher, whenever necessary, can recommend to the school board that you be *expelled* from school. When you are expelled, you are not allowed to return to school.

The laws that relate to you at work have been established to protect you from *oppressive child labor practices*. This means it is against the law for you to do work that is in any way cruel or dangerous.

This was the way things were before child labor laws:

Today's child labor laws make it against the law for you to work at jobs that could possibly damage you physically or mentally. Here are some jobs that the law considers cruel or dangerous:

- activities that expose workers to radioactive substances
- coal mining
- mining other than coal mining
- dangerous exhibitions like certain circus acts
- driving a motor vehicle
- excavation and certain agricultural activities
- logging and sawmill activities
- manufacturing brick and tile
- manufacturing and storing explosives

- operation of baking machines
- operation of paper-product machines
- operation of power-driven, hoisting apparatus
- operation of power-driven, metal-forming machines
- operation of power-driven saws and shears
- power-driven wood working
- roofing
- slaughtering and meat packing
- street selling
- wrecking and demolition

If you are 14 or 15 years old, you can work outside of school hours if

- you do not work at night and
- you do not work too many hours.

You must be 16 years of age or older to have a *full-time job* (a job in which a person works at least 40 hours per week).

Anyone working full-time must receive a *minimum wage* or more for his or her services. A minimum wage is an amount of money the law requires an employer (boss) to pay an employee (worker).

This chart shows you how many hours you are allowed to work when you are fourteen, fifteen, and sixteen years old:

CHiLD'S AGE	MAXiMUM WORK HOURS	
	School in session	School NOT in session
14-and 15- year-olds	3 hrs./day 18 hrs./week	8 hrs./day 40 hrs./week*
16-year-olds	4 hrs./day 20 hrs./week	8 hrs./day 48 hrs./week**

* No overtime allowed

** The 8 additional hours allowed during a week must be paid at an adult overtime rate. These can only occur during an additional day.

I WONDER IF THIS PERTAINS TO DOGS.

There is no age or time limit on doing odd jobs in private homes such as household chores, yard work, or baby-sitting. In other words, anyone can do these jobs and be paid for them.

Also, children of any age can do agricultural work as long as it is not dangerous.

In regard to **work permits,** in many states children under 16 years of age are required to have a "permit to work" to work at jobs other than odd jobs in private homes or on farms. Usually, the permit is issued by a school authority who evaluates the situation and decides that working will not interfere with the child's education.

In many states employers must have a **permit to employ** in order to hire children under 16 years of age. This is to make sure that the work and the working conditions provided by the employer are suitable for children.

The laws you have learned about in this book have been established so that you and the people around you can lead safe, productive lives. For this reason. . .